SEX EDUCATION FOR 8-12 YEARS OLDS

Let's Talk About How Growing Child Should Take Ownership Of Their Body; Understanding Puberty and Digital Safety

BY

MABLE JOHNSON

TABLE OF CONTENTS

INTRODUCTION

Sex education for 8-12-year-olds is a delicate yet essential aspect of their development. It's a time when children are beginning to form their understanding of the world around them, including their own bodies and the concept of relationships. Approaching this topic with care, respect, and age-appropriate information is crucial in empowering children to make informed decisions, develop healthy attitudes towards their bodies, and navigate relationships safely as they grow older.

At this stage, children are curious and naturally seek answers to their questions about their bodies and the changes they're experiencing. Providing accurate and accessible information helps demystify these changes and fosters a

4

sense of comfort and confidence in their own skin. Sex education for this age group typically focuses on foundational concepts such as anatomy, puberty, reproduction, and the importance of consent.

Understanding their own bodies is key to self-awareness and self-confidence. Teaching children about anatomy in a clear and factual manner helps them develop a healthy body image and a sense of ownership over their own bodies. Learning correct anatomical terms also enables effective communication about their bodies, which is essential for seeking help when needed and setting boundaries in interpersonal relationships.

Puberty is a significant milestone in a child's life, and providing education about it beforehand can help alleviate anxiety and confusion. Explaining the physical and emotional changes that come with puberty, such as growth spurts, menstruation, and hormonal fluctuations, can empower children to embrace these changes as a natural part of growing up rather than something to be feared or ashamed of.

Reproduction is another important topic to address in sex education for 8-12-year-olds. While the details may be simplified, introducing the basics of how babies are conceived and born lays the groundwork for a deeper understanding of human sexuality later on. It's important to emphasize that reproduction is a natural process that occurs within the context of consensual, loving relationships.

Teaching children about consent is perhaps one of the most critical aspects of sex education at any age. At 8-12 years old, children are beginning to navigate friendships and social interactions more independently, making it essential to instill the importance of respecting personal boundaries and seeking consent in all interactions. Teaching them to recognize and assert their own boundaries while respecting those of others sets the foundation for healthy relationships built on mutual respect and understanding.

Sex education for 8-12-year-olds should be approached with sensitivity, honesty, and inclusivity. It's important to create a safe and supportive environment where children feel comfortable asking questions and expressing their thoughts and feelings. Recognizing and respecting the diversity of experiences and identities within the classroom is also essential, ensuring that all children feel seen, valued, and included in the conversation.

Ultimately, sex education for 8-12-year-olds sets the stage for a lifetime of healthy decision-making, positive self-image, and respectful relationships. By providing accurate information, fostering open communication, and promoting values of respect and consent, educators and caregivers can empower children to navigate the complexities of sexuality and relationships with confidence and integrity.

CHAPTER 1: UNDERSTANDING OUR BODIES

The Basics of Anatomy

As we grow up, it's important to learn about our bodies and how they work. Understanding our anatomy helps us take care of ourselves and make healthy choices. Let's explore the basics of anatomy in a way that's easy to understand.

Our Body Parts: We all have different body parts that serve different purposes. Some parts are for seeing, hearing, smelling, tasting, and feeling. Other parts are for moving, like our arms and legs. It's essential to know the names of these body parts so we can communicate about them accurately.

Boys and Girls: Boys and girls have some body parts that are the same and some that are different. Both boys and girls have a heart, lungs, bones, and muscles. But boys have a penis and testicles, while girls have a vagina, ovaries, and uterus. These parts are essential for reproduction, which is how babies are made.

Puberty: As we grow older, our bodies go through changes called puberty. Puberty usually starts around the ages of 8 to 10 for some children. During puberty, our bodies start to develop adult features like growing taller, growing hair in new places, and our reproductive organs start to mature. This is a natural process, and everyone goes through it at their own pace.

Respecting Our Bodies: It's essential to respect and take care of our bodies. This means keeping them clean, eating healthy foods, getting enough sleep, and exercising regularly. It also means understanding that our bodies belong to us, and no one should make us feel uncomfortable or unsafe with our bodies.

Private Parts: Some parts of our bodies are private, which means they are not for anyone else to touch or see without our permission. These include our genitals, buttocks, and breasts. It's important to know that if anyone tries to touch or look at our private parts in a way that makes us feel uncomfortable, we should tell a trusted adult right away.

Asking Questions: It's normal to have questions about our bodies, and it's okay to ask them. We can talk to our parents, teachers, or other trusted adults when we have questions or need help understanding something. They are there to support us and provide accurate information.

Understanding our bodies is an essential part of growing up. By learning about our anatomy and how our bodies work, we can make informed choices and take care of ourselves better. Remember, our bodies are amazing, and it's essential to treat them with kindness and respect.

Embracing Changes: Puberty

As children grow older, their bodies go through many changes. This is a natural part of growing up called puberty. Puberty is a time when your body develops from a child's body into an adult's body. It's a time of excitement, but it can also be a bit confusing. Understanding these changes is important, so let's explore them together.

What is Puberty?

Puberty is a time when your body starts to change in many ways. It usually happens between the ages of 8 and 14 for girls, and 9 and 15 for boys, but everyone is different. These changes happen because your body is preparing to become capable of having babies when you're older.

Physical Changes:

Girls: You might notice your breasts start to grow. This is normal and happens to all girls during puberty. Your body will also start to produce eggs, which means you'll have periods.

Boys: Boys will notice their testicles and penis get larger. Hair will start to grow under the arms and around the genitals. Boys will also start producing sperm, which is needed to make babies.

Emotional Changes:

During puberty, you might feel lots of different emotions. Sometimes you might feel happy, excited, or full of energy, while other times you might feel sad, angry, or even confused. These emotions are all normal and part of growing up. Talking to someone you trust, like a parent or teacher, can help you understand and cope with these feelings.

Personal Hygiene:

With all these changes happening, it's important to take care of your body. This means showering regularly, using deodorant to prevent body odor, and washing your face to prevent pimples. Taking care of your body helps you feel good about yourself and stay healthy.

Understanding Consent and Boundaries:

It's crucial to understand that nobody should ever touch you in a way that makes you feel uncomfortable. You have the right to say no to any touch that doesn't feel right, even if it's from someone you know. Always speak up if you feel uncomfortable or unsafe, and tell a trusted adult.

Respecting Others' Bodies:

Just as it's important for others to respect your body, it's equally important for you to respect theirs. Always ask for permission before touching someone else, and never make fun of or tease others about their bodies or the changes they're going through.

Communication with Parents or Guardians:

Your parents or guardians are there to help you understand these changes and answer any questions you might have. Don't be afraid to talk to them about puberty. They want to support you and make sure you feel comfortable and informed.

Remember, puberty is a natural part of growing up, and everyone goes through it at their own pace. Embracing these changes and understanding your body is an important step towards becoming a confident and healthy adult. If you ever have questions or concerns, don't hesitate to reach out to a trusted adult for guidance and support.

Respecting Personal Boundaries

As children grow and develop, it's natural for them to have questions about their bodies and the changes they're experiencing. Understanding our bodies and respecting personal boundaries are crucial aspects of growing up and navigating the world around us. In this guide, we'll explore the importance of sex education for children aged 8 to 10, focusing on empowering them with knowledge while instilling a sense of respect for themselves and others.

Understanding Our Bodies:

Our bodies are amazing and complex, and it's essential for children to understand the basics of how their bodies work. From the different body parts to the changes that occur during puberty, here are some key points to cover:

Body Parts: Teach children the names of their body parts, including the genitals, and explain their functions in simple, age-appropriate language. Encourage open communication and assure them that it's okay to ask questions about their bodies.

Puberty: Explain that puberty is a natural process that occurs as they grow older. Discuss the physical changes that occur during puberty, such as growth spurts, the development of breasts and testicles, and the appearance of body hair. Emphasize that these changes are normal and part of growing up.

Reproduction: Introduce the concept of reproduction in a simple manner, explaining how babies are made through the combination of an egg from the mother and sperm from the father.

19

Use diagrams or illustrations to help children visualize the process.

Respecting Personal Boundaries:

Respecting personal boundaries is an essential aspect of healthy relationships and self-respect. Teach children about the importance of setting and respecting boundaries, both for themselves and others. Here are some key points to cover:

Consent: Explain the concept of consent by emphasizing that it's important to ask for permission before touching someone else and to respect their answer, whether it's yes or no. Teach children that they have the right to say no to any physical contact that makes them uncomfortable.

Privacy: Discuss the importance of privacy when it comes to their bodies. Encourage children to respect their own privacy by not sharing intimate details about their bodies with others and to respect the privacy of others by not touching or looking at someone else's private areas without permission.

Safe Touch vs. Unsafe Touch: Teach children the difference between safe touches, such as hugs from family members or high-fives from friends, and unsafe touches, such as unwanted touching or groping. Empower them to trust their instincts and speak up if they ever feel uncomfortable or unsafe.

By providing children with age-appropriate sex education and teaching them to respect personal boundaries, we can empower them to navigate the world with confidence and self-respect. Encourage open communication, answer their questions honestly, and create a safe and supportive environment where they feel comfortable discussing sensitive topics. Remember, educating children about their bodies and boundaries is a vital step in helping them develop healthy relationships and attitudes towards themselves and others.

CHAPTER 2: HEALTHY RELATIONSHIPS

Building Trust and Communication

Understanding healthy relationships is an essential part of growing up. As you navigate through life, you'll encounter various relationships with family, friends, and eventually, romantic partners. Learning about trust and communication lays the foundation for building strong, respectful connections with others.

Building Trust:

Trust is like a delicate seed that needs care and attention to grow. In healthy relationships, trust forms the basis of mutual respect and understanding. Here's how you can cultivate trust:

Honesty: Always be truthful with others, even when it's difficult. Honesty builds credibility and shows that you value the relationship.

Reliability: Keep your promises and follow through on your commitments. Being dependable helps others feel secure in your relationship.

Respect: Treat others the way you want to be treated. Respect their feelings, opinions, and boundaries.

Openness: Share your thoughts and feelings openly with trusted individuals. Being transparent fosters a sense of closeness and intimacy.

Communication:

Effective communication is the cornerstone of any healthy relationship. It involves both speaking and listening with empathy and understanding. Here are some tips for improving communication:

Active Listening: Pay attention when others speak. Show that you're listening by making eye contact, nodding, and asking questions to clarify your understanding.

Expressing Feelings: Learn to express your feelings in a constructive way. Use "I" statements to communicate how you feel without blaming others.

Empathy: Put yourself in the other person's shoes to understand their perspective.

Empathizing with their feelings helps strengthen your bond.

Problem-Solving: Work together to find solutions to conflicts or disagreements. Focus on finding common ground and compromising when necessary.

Practicing Consent:

Consent is a crucial aspect of any relationship, including friendships and romantic partnerships. It means that all parties involved freely agree to participate in any activity, whether it's holding hands, hugging, or something more intimate. Here's what consent looks like:

Clear Communication: Ask for consent before engaging in any physical activity. Respect the other person's answer, whether it's yes or no.

Mutual Agreement: Both parties should willingly agree to participate without feeling pressured or coerced.

Respect Boundaries: Understand and respect each other's boundaries. If someone says no or feels uncomfortable, honor their decision without question.

Learning about trust, communication, and consent sets the stage for healthy relationships in all areas of your life. By practicing these skills, you'll build strong connections based on mutual respect, understanding, and empathy. Remember, healthy relationships are built on a foundation of trust, open communication, and mutual respect, and they enrich our lives in countless ways.

Recognizing Consent and Respect

Welcome, young friend! As you grow up, you'll hear a lot about relationships, friendships, and all sorts of feelings. It's essential to understand how to build healthy relationships based on respect and consent. Let's embark on this journey together!

Understanding Healthy Relationships:

Healthy relationships are like gardens. They need care, respect, and understanding to flourish. In a healthy relationship, both people feel safe, happy, and respected. Whether it's with friends, family, or even pets, treating each other with kindness and consideration is key.

What is Consent?

Consent means agreeing to something freely and willingly. Just like sharing toys or playing games, it's crucial to respect each other's boundaries. If someone says no to something, it's important to listen and understand. Remember, your body and your feelings belong to you, and you have the right to say no if something makes you uncomfortable.

Recognizing Consent:

Consent can be shown in many ways, such as saying "yes," smiling, or giving a high five. But remember, it's not just about words; it's also about paying attention to how someone feels. If someone seems unsure or uncomfortable, it's essential to stop and check if everything is okay. Always ask before giving hugs, borrowing things, or playing rough games.

Respecting Boundaries:

Boundaries are like invisible lines that show what's okay and what's not. It's essential to respect other people's boundaries and to communicate yours clearly. If someone tells you they don't like something, like being tickled or teased, it's important to listen and stop. And if you're not sure, it's okay to ask!

Communication is Key:

Talking openly and honestly is crucial in any relationship. If something is bothering you or making you feel uncomfortable, it's important to speak up. Likewise, listen carefully when others talk to you. Understanding each other's feelings helps build trust and respect.

Remember, building healthy relationships takes time and effort. It's okay to make mistakes along the way; what matters is that you learn from them. Always treat others how you would like to be treated, with kindness, respect, and understanding. Keep nurturing those healthy relationships, and watch them bloom beautifully!

Navigating Friendships and Peer Pressure

Welcome, young explorer, to the fascinating journey of understanding healthy relationships! As you grow and discover more about the world around you, it's essential to learn about friendships, peer pressure, and how to maintain positive connections with others. In this guide, we'll explore what it means to have healthy relationships and how to navigate through friendships and peer pressure with confidence and respect.

Understanding Healthy Relationships:

First things first, let's talk about what makes a relationship healthy. Healthy relationships are built on trust, respect, communication, and kindness. Just like a garden needs sunlight and water to grow, friendships need nurturing and care to thrive. In a healthy relationship, you feel safe, heard, and valued for who you are.

Navigating Friendships:

Friendships are like treasures; they bring joy, laughter, and companionship into our lives. But just like any treasure, they require careful navigation. Here are some tips for building and maintaining healthy friendships:

Be Yourself: The best friendships are formed when you're true to yourself. Don't be afraid to show your quirks and unique qualities.

Choose Wisely: Surround yourself with friends who uplift and support you. Look for people who share similar interests and values.

Communication is Key: Talk openly with your friends about how you feel and listen to their thoughts and feelings too. Good communication helps solve problems and strengthens bonds.

Respect Boundaries: Everyone has boundaries, and it's essential to respect them. If a friend says no to something, accept their decision gracefully.

Resolve Conflicts Peacefully: Disagreements are a natural part of any relationship. Learn to resolve conflicts calmly and respectfully, without resorting to hurtful words or actions.

Navigating Peer Pressure:

Peer pressure is when friends or classmates try to influence you to do something you're not comfortable with. It's normal to feel pressure from peers, but it's essential to stay true to yourself. Here's how to handle peer pressure:

Trust Your Instincts: If something doesn't feel right to you, it's okay to say no. Trust your instincts and stand firm in your decisions.

Choose Friends Wisely: Surround yourself with friends who respect your choices and don't pressure you into doing things you're uncomfortable with.

Practice Assertiveness: Assertiveness means standing up for yourself in a calm and confident manner. Practice saying no firmly but politely when faced with peer pressure.

Seek Support: If you're struggling with peer pressure, don't be afraid to seek support from a trusted adult, like a parent, teacher, or school counselor. They can offer guidance and help you navigate challenging situations.

Navigating friendships and peer pressure can sometimes feel like a tricky maze, but with the right tools and mindset, you can emerge stronger and more confident. Remember, healthy relationships are built on trust, respect, and communication. Stay true to yourself, surround yourself with supportive friends, and don't be afraid to seek help when needed. You've got this!

CHAPTER 3:
REPRODUCTIVE HEALTH

Exploring Reproduction and Fertility

Understanding reproductive health and fertility is an essential part of growing up. As you begin to explore the changes happening in your body, it's natural to have questions. This guide aims to provide you with valuable information about reproduction, fertility, and sexual health, empowering you to make informed decisions and take care of your body.

What is Reproduction?

Reproduction is the process by which living organisms produce offspring. In humans, reproduction involves the combination of a male's sperm and a female's egg, leading to the development of a new life. This process

37

typically occurs through sexual intercourse, but there are other methods, such as assisted reproductive technologies, for individuals who may face challenges in conceiving naturally.

Understanding Your Reproductive Organs:

For females, the reproductive organs include the ovaries, fallopian tubes, uterus, and vagina. The ovaries produce eggs, which are released monthly during ovulation. The fallopian tubes are where fertilization takes place when sperm meets the egg. The fertilized egg then implants itself in the uterus, where it grows and develops into a baby. The vagina is the passageway through which menstrual blood exits the body and where a baby passes through during childbirth.

For males, the reproductive organs include the testes, epididymis, vas deferens, and penis. The testes produce sperm, which is stored and matured in the epididymis. During ejaculation, sperm travels through the vas deferens and mixes with seminal fluid to form semen, which is ejaculated through the penis during sexual intercourse.

Menstruation:

Menstruation, commonly known as a period, is a natural process that occurs in females typically every 28 days. During menstruation, the lining of the uterus sheds, resulting in the discharge of blood from the vagina. This process is a sign that the female body is capable of reproduction, but it does not necessarily mean that pregnancy has occurred.

Understanding Fertility:

Fertility refers to the ability to conceive and produce offspring. Both males and females have a finite window of fertility, with peak fertility occurring during specific stages of life. In females, fertility typically begins with the onset of menstruation (menarche) and declines gradually with age, especially after the age of 35. In males, fertility can be affected by factors such as age, health, and lifestyle choices.

Protecting Your Reproductive Health:

Taking care of your reproductive health is important for your overall well-being. Here are some tips to help you maintain a healthy reproductive system:

Practice safe sex: Use condoms to protect against sexually transmitted infections (STIs) and unintended pregnancies.

Communicate openly: Talk to a trusted adult or healthcare provider about any questions or concerns you may have about your reproductive health.

Stay informed: Educate yourself about reproductive health, fertility, and contraception to make informed decisions.

Eat a balanced diet: Consuming nutritious foods can support reproductive health and hormone balance.

Stay active: Regular exercise can help maintain a healthy weight and promote overall well-being.

Understanding reproduction, fertility, and sexual health is an important part of growing up. By learning about your body and how it works, you can take control of your reproductive health and make informed decisions. Remember, it's normal to have questions, and there are always trusted adults and healthcare providers available to support you along the way.

Menstruation: A Natural Process

As children grow, they start to notice changes happening in their bodies and may have questions about what's happening. One essential aspect of growing up is understanding reproductive health, including menstruation. It's important to approach this topic with openness, honesty, and age-appropriate information. Let's explore menstruation as a natural process in the journey of reproductive health.

Understanding Menstruation:

Menstruation, often referred to as a period, is a natural process that happens in the bodies of people assigned female at birth. It usually begins around the ages of 10 to 15, but each person is different. During menstruation, the body sheds blood and tissue from the uterus through the vagina. This process typically occurs once a month and lasts for a few days.

Why Does Menstruation Happen?

Menstruation is a sign that a person's body is healthy and capable of reproduction. Each month, the uterus prepares for a possible pregnancy by thickening its lining with blood and tissue. If pregnancy doesn't occur, the body no longer needs this extra lining, so it sheds it through menstruation.

Common Questions About Menstruation:

Children may have many questions about menstruation. Here are some common ones and their answers:

Is it Normal to Feel Nervous or Scared?

Yes, it's normal to feel nervous or scared about menstruation, especially if it's something new. But remember, it's a natural process that happens to many people, and there's nothing to be ashamed of.

Does Menstruation Hurt?

Some people experience cramps or discomfort during their periods, while others may not feel anything at all. If someone experiences severe pain, they should talk to a trusted adult or healthcare provider.

Can I Swim or Play Sports During My Period?

Absolutely! Menstruation shouldn't stop anyone from doing the activities they enjoy. Using period products like tampons or menstrual cups can make swimming and sports more comfortable.

Will Everyone Know When I'm on My Period?

No, menstruation is a private matter, and it's entirely up to each person whether they want to share that information or not. Wearing period products like pads or tampons helps keep it discreet.

What If I'm Not Ready for My Period?

It's normal to feel unprepared for menstruation, but it's essential to be informed. Talk to a parent, guardian, or trusted adult about what to expect and how to manage periods when they start.

Menstruation is a natural part of reproductive health for people assigned female at birth. Understanding this process and being informed can help children feel more confident and prepared as they grow up. Encouraging open communication and providing accurate information ensures that children develop a healthy attitude towards their bodies and menstruation. Remember, it's all part of growing up!

Understanding Conception and Birth

Welcome, young explorer! Today, we embark on an exciting journey to understand a crucial aspect of our bodies: reproductive health. We'll dive into the fascinating world of conception and birth, unraveling the mysteries of how life begins and the incredible journey a baby takes before entering the world.

What is Reproductive Health?

Reproductive health is all about our bodies' ability to reproduce and give birth to new life. It involves understanding how our reproductive organs work and how babies are created.

Understanding Conception:

Conception is the magical moment when a sperm cell from a man joins with an egg cell from a woman to create a new life. This usually happens during a process called "sexual intercourse," where the man's sperm travels through the woman's body to meet the egg.

Let's Meet the Players:

Sperm: These tiny cells come from the man's body. They're like little swimmers racing to reach the egg.

Egg: The egg comes from the woman's body. It's like a cozy home waiting for the sperm to arrive. Uterus: This is where the fertilized egg attaches and grows into a baby. It's like a safe, warm nest for the baby to develop.

Fallopian Tubes: These are like tunnels connecting the ovaries (where the eggs are stored) to the uterus. They're the pathway for the sperm to reach the egg.

The Journey of the Egg and Sperm:

When a man and woman decide to have a baby, the man's sperm travels through his penis and into the woman's vagina. From there, they swim through the cervix (the opening of the uterus) and into the fallopian tubes, where they hope to meet an egg. If one lucky sperm manages to find and penetrate the egg, fertilization occurs, and a new life begins!

The Miracle of Birth:

Once the egg is fertilized, it starts to divide and grow. It attaches itself to the lining of the uterus and continues to develop into a baby over the next nine months. This journey is called pregnancy. When the baby is fully developed and ready to enter the world, the mother goes into labor. During labor, the baby moves through the birth canal (the passage between the uterus and the outside of the body) and is born into the world!

Understanding conception and birth is a beautiful and natural part of life. By learning about our bodies and how they work, we gain a deeper appreciation for the miracle of life. Remember, it's essential to ask questions and talk to trusted adults if you ever have any concerns or want to learn more about reproductive health. Keep exploring, and never stop seeking knowledge!

CHAPTER 4: SEXUALITY AND GENDER

Embracing Diversity and Inclusion

Understanding sexuality and gender is an important part of growing up. As you grow older, you might have questions about your body, feelings, and relationships. It's okay to have these questions, and it's important to learn about sexuality and gender in a safe and supportive environment.

What is Sexuality?

Sexuality is a big word that includes many things about who you are and how you feel. It's about the feelings you have for other people, how you see yourself, and how your body works. Everyone's sexuality is unique and special, just like you are.

Gender Identity:

Gender identity is about how you feel inside and how you see yourself as a boy, girl, both, or neither. Some people are born boys and feel like boys, and some are born girls and feel like girls. But some people might feel like they are both a boy and a girl, or neither. It's essential to know that there are many different ways to be a boy, girl, or anything else, and all of them are perfectly okay.

Embracing Diversity:

Just like there are many different colors in a rainbow, there are many different kinds of people in the world. It's essential to respect and accept everyone, no matter how they look, who they love, or how they identify. Being kind and inclusive means treating everyone with love and understanding.

54

Love and Relationships:

As you get older, you might start to have feelings for other people. It's natural to have crushes or feel attracted to someone else. Remember that it's essential to always respect other people's feelings and boundaries. Healthy relationships are built on trust, communication, and mutual respect.

Body Changes:

As you grow older, your body will start to change. This is a natural part of growing up, and everyone goes through it. It's essential to take care of your body by eating healthy foods, exercising, and getting enough rest. If you have any questions about the changes happening to your body, don't hesitate to ask a trusted adult or a healthcare provider.

Understanding sexuality and gender is an ongoing journey that lasts a lifetime. It's okay to have questions and feelings about these topics, and it's important to find safe and supportive spaces to explore them. Remember always to be kind, inclusive, and respectful of yourself and others. By embracing diversity and inclusion, we can create a world where everyone feels accepted and loved for who they are.

Exploring Sexual Orientation

Understanding sexuality and gender is an important part of growing up and becoming a well-rounded individual. As children begin to explore their identities and the world around them, it's essential to provide them with accurate information and support. In this guide, we will explore the concepts of sexuality and gender in a way that is age-appropriate and easy to understand for children between the ages of 8 and 10.

What is Sexuality?

Sexuality refers to the feelings, attractions, and behaviors that make each person unique. It's about who we are attracted to and how we express those feelings. Everyone experiences sexuality differently, and there is no right or wrong way to feel.

Understanding Sexual Orientation:

One aspect of sexuality is sexual orientation, which is who we are attracted to romantically or sexually. There are different sexual orientations, and it's okay to feel attracted to people of the same gender, different genders, or any gender.

Heterosexuality: Some people are attracted to people of the opposite gender. For example, a boy may feel attracted to a girl, and vice versa.

Homosexuality: Some people are attracted to people of the same gender. For example, a girl may feel attracted to another girl, and vice versa.

Bisexuality: Some people are attracted to people of more than one gender. For example, someone who is bisexual may feel attracted to both boys and girls.

Pansexuality: Some people are attracted to people regardless of their gender. For example, someone who is pansexual may feel attracted to boys, girls, or people who identify as non-binary or transgender.

It's important to remember that everyone's feelings and experiences are valid, and there is no right or wrong way to be attracted to others.

Understanding Gender:

Gender is different from biological sex and refers to the roles, behaviors, and identities that society considers appropriate for boys, girls, men, and women. While many people identify as the gender they were assigned at birth (based on their physical body), some people may identify as a different gender, or they may not identify strictly as male or female.

Cisgender: A person who identifies with the gender they were assigned at birth is called cisgender. For example, someone who was labeled male at birth and identifies as a boy is cisgender.

Transgender: Some people may feel that the gender they were assigned at birth does not match who they are on the inside. These individuals are transgender. For example, someone who was labeled male at birth but identifies as a girl is transgender.

Non-binary: Some people do not identify strictly as male or female. They may feel that they are both genders, neither gender, or something else entirely. These individuals are non-binary.

It's important to respect everyone's gender identity and use the pronouns that they prefer.

Exploring sexuality and gender can be a complex journey, but it's an important part of understanding ourselves and the world around us. By learning about different sexual orientations and gender identities, we can create a more inclusive and accepting society where everyone feels valued and respected for who they are. Remember, it's okay to ask questions and seek support from trusted adults if you ever feel confused or unsure.

Understanding Gender Identity

Understanding ourselves and others is an important part of growing up. As you grow, you might have questions about who you are and how you fit into the world. One aspect of this is gender identity, which is all about how you feel inside about being a boy, a girl, both, or neither. Let's explore this together!

What is Gender Identity?

Gender identity is how you feel inside about whether you are a boy, a girl, both, or neither. For most people, their gender identity matches the sex they were assigned at birth. This means if a doctor said "It's a boy!" when you were born, and you feel like a boy, then your gender identity matches your biological sex. But for some people, their gender identity might be different from what they were told at birth. And that's perfectly okay!

Understanding Different Gender Identities:
There are many different ways people might experience their gender identity. Here are some terms you might hear:

Cisgender: This is when your gender identity matches the sex you were assigned at birth. For example, if you were born a girl and feel like a girl, you are cisgender.

Transgender: Some people feel like they are a different gender than the one they were assigned at birth. For example, someone who was assigned male at birth but feels like a girl is transgender.

Non-Binary: Some people feel like they are neither strictly a boy nor strictly a girl. They might feel like a mix of both genders, or they might feel like neither. This is called being non-binary.

Gender-Fluid: Some people feel like their gender identity can change over time. One day they might feel more like a boy, and another day they might feel more like a girl. This is called being gender-fluid.

Genderqueer: This is an umbrella term that can include many different gender identities that don't fit into the traditional categories of male or female.

It's important to remember that everyone's experience of gender identity is unique, and it's okay to be different!

Respecting Everyone's Gender Identity:

Just like we should respect people for who they are on the inside, we should also respect their gender identity. This means using the name and pronouns that someone prefers, even if they are different from what you might expect. For example, if someone tells you they are a girl, you should call them "she" and "her," even if they were assigned male at birth.

It's also important to remember that it's not polite to ask someone about their body or their private parts. Everyone's body is different, and it's not okay to make assumptions about someone based on how they look.

Understanding gender identity is an important part of respecting and accepting others for who they are. By learning about different gender identities and being respectful of people's feelings, we can create a world where everyone feels accepted and valued for who they are. Keep asking questions and learning more about yourself and the world around you!

CHAPTER 5: SAFETY AND BOUNDARIES

Setting Personal Boundaries

Understanding safety and boundaries is essential as you grow up. Just like you have rules to stay safe when crossing the road or playing with friends, there are rules to keep you safe and comfortable in other parts of your life, including learning about your body and relationships. Let's explore how you can set personal boundaries and stay safe when it comes to sex education.

Understanding Safety:

Safety means feeling secure and protected in different situations. When it comes to sex education, safety is about making sure you feel comfortable and respected when talking or learning about your body and relationships. It's important to know that you can talk to trusted adults about anything that makes you feel confused, uncomfortable, or scared.

Setting Personal Boundaries:

Personal boundaries are like invisible lines that you draw around yourself to protect your body, feelings, and personal space. Here are some ways you can set and respect your personal boundaries:

Know Your Body: Understanding your body and what feels comfortable or uncomfortable is the first step in setting boundaries. You can learn about your body through books, talks with trusted adults, or reputable websites.

Identify Your Limits: Think about what you feel okay with and what you don't when it comes to touch, conversations, and personal space. Your boundaries might be different from others, and that's perfectly okay.

Speak Up: If someone makes you feel uncomfortable or tries to cross your boundaries, it's essential to speak up. You can say things like, "Stop, I don't like that," or "That makes me uncomfortable." Remember, your feelings and boundaries are valid.

Respect Others' Boundaries: Just like you want others to respect your boundaries, it's important to respect theirs too. Always ask for permission before touching someone else, and listen carefully if they say no or seem uncomfortable.

Trust Your Instincts: If something doesn't feel right, trust your instincts and remove yourself from the situation. You have the right to feel safe and comfortable at all times.

Talk to Trusted Adults: If you're unsure about something or need help understanding boundaries, talk to a trusted adult, like a parent, teacher, or family member. They are there to support you and answer your questions.

Understanding safety and boundaries is an important part of growing up and staying safe. By knowing your body, setting personal boundaries, and speaking up when you feel uncomfortable, you can navigate sex education and relationships with confidence and respect for yourself and others. Remember, you deserve to feel safe, respected, and valued always.

Recognizing and Responding to Unsafe Situations

Sex education is an essential aspect of growing up, and learning about safety and boundaries is crucial for children aged 8 to 10. Understanding how to recognize and respond to unsafe situations empowers children to protect themselves and seek help when needed. Here's a guide to help children navigate safety and boundaries:

Understanding Safe and Unsafe Touches

Start by explaining that everyone has a right to their own body, and no one should touch them in a way that makes them feel uncomfortable.

Teach them about safe, appropriate touches, like hugs from family members or high fives from friends.

Explain that if anyone touches them in a way that feels strange, uncomfortable, or secret, they should speak up and tell a trusted adult immediately.

Recognizing Unsafe Situations

Help children identify behaviors or situations that may feel unsafe. This could include someone asking them to keep a secret, touching them in private areas, or making them feel scared or uncomfortable.

Encourage children to trust their instincts. If something doesn't feel right, it's important to speak up and seek help.

Setting Boundaries

Teach children how to set personal boundaries by saying "no" firmly and confidently if someone tries to touch them inappropriately or makes them feel uncomfortable.

Explain that it's okay to say "no" even to adults or older children if they are crossing boundaries.

Reassure them that they won't get in trouble for speaking up and setting boundaries.

Seeking Help

Emphasize the importance of seeking help from a trusted adult if they ever feel unsafe or uncomfortable. Trusted adults may include parents, teachers, school counselors, or family members.

Encourage open communication by letting children know that they can talk to you about anything, even if it feels scary or embarrassing.

Remind children that they are not alone and that there are people who care about their safety and well-being.

Practicing Safety Strategies

Role-play different scenarios with your child to help them practice what to do if they encounter an unsafe situation. This could include saying "no," walking away, and seeking help from a trusted adult.

Teach children about safe adults in their community, such as police officers or firefighters, who they can turn to for help if needed.

By teaching children about safety and boundaries, we empower them to protect themselves and navigate the world with confidence. Encourage ongoing conversations about these topics and provide support and reassurance as they learn to recognize and respond to unsafe situations. Together, we can help children develop the skills they need to stay safe and healthy.

Online Safety and Digital Citizenship

In today's world, the internet plays a big part in our lives. It's where we learn, play, and connect with others. But just like the real world, there are things we need to be aware of to stay safe and protected online. This guide is here to help you understand how to navigate the digital world safely and set healthy boundaries for yourself.

Understanding Online Safety:

Personal Information: Always remember that not everyone online is who they say they are. Never share personal information like your full name, address, phone number, or school name with strangers online. Your safety is the most important thing.

Privacy Settings: Many websites and apps have privacy settings that allow you to control who can see your information and posts. Take some time to learn about these settings and adjust them to keep your information private.

Stranger Danger: Just like in real life, it's important to be cautious when talking to strangers online. If someone you don't know tries to chat with you or befriend you, it's okay to ignore them and tell a trusted adult.

Cyberbullying: Bullying doesn't just happen on the playground—it can happen online too. If someone is being mean to you online, don't respond. Instead, talk to a trusted adult about what's happening and how you're feeling.

Setting Boundaries:

Time Limits: Spending too much time online can be unhealthy. Set limits for yourself on how much time you spend online each day and make sure to take breaks to do other activities like playing outside or reading a book.

Content Filters: Not everything online is appropriate for kids. Ask your parents to set up content filters or parental controls on your devices to block inappropriate content.

Respecting Others' Boundaries: Just like you have boundaries, other people do too. Always ask for permission before sharing someone else's photos, videos, or personal information online.

Trust Your Instincts: If something online makes you feel uncomfortable or uneasy, trust your instincts and talk to a trusted adult about it. It's always better to be safe than sorry.

Remember, the internet can be a fun and exciting place, but it's important to use it responsibly and safely. By understanding online safety and setting healthy boundaries for yourself, you can enjoy all the benefits of the digital world while staying protected from potential risks.

CHAPTER 6: MEDIA LITERACY

Critically Analyzing Media Portrayals

In today's world, children are exposed to various forms of media that often portray relationships, intimacy, and sexuality. As parents and educators, it's crucial to equip children aged 8 to 10 with the skills to critically analyze these portrayals. By fostering media literacy within the realm of sex education, we can empower children to make informed decisions and develop healthy attitudes towards sexuality.

Understanding Media Portrayals:

Media, including television shows, movies, advertisements, and social media, often present unrealistic or exaggerated depictions of relationships and sexuality. Characters may engage in behaviors or situations that are not appropriate for children their age. It's essential to help children recognize these discrepancies and understand that media portrayals do not always reflect real-life experiences.

Questioning Stereotypes:

Encourage children to question stereotypes perpetuated by the media. Discuss how gender roles and expectations are often portrayed and how they may not accurately represent the diversity of human experiences. By challenging stereotypes, children can develop more inclusive and respectful attitudes towards others.

Identifying Healthy Relationships:

Guide children in recognizing the characteristics of healthy relationships portrayed in the media. Emphasize the importance of mutual respect, communication, consent, and boundaries. Help them understand that healthy relationships involve equality and support rather than control or manipulation.

Addressing Sexualization:

Discuss how the media sometimes sexualizes individuals, particularly women and girls. Teach children to recognize when this occurs and how it can contribute to unrealistic beauty standards and harmful attitudes towards sexuality. Encourage them to value people for their personalities, talents, and character rather than their physical appearance.

Navigating Peer Pressure:

Explain to children how media portrayals can influence peer pressure regarding relationships and sexuality. Encourage open communication about peer influences and provide strategies for making independent and informed choices. Teach them to assert their boundaries and resist pressure to engage in behaviors they are uncomfortable with.

Promoting Critical Thinking:

Above all, encourage children to think critically about the media they consume. Teach them to ask questions, analyze messages, and consider different perspectives. By developing these skills, children can become more discerning consumers of media and make choices that align with their values and beliefs.

By integrating media literacy into sex education for 8 to 10-year-olds, we can empower children to navigate the complex landscape of media portrayals of relationships and sexuality.

Through critical analysis and thoughtful discussion, we can help children develop healthy attitudes, respect for themselves and others, and the skills to make informed decisions in the digital age.

Understanding Advertising and Stereotypes

Sex education is an essential aspect of a child's development, providing them with the knowledge and skills to navigate their changing bodies, relationships, and the world around them. In today's digital age, media plays a significant role in shaping perceptions and attitudes towards sex and relationships. Understanding advertising and stereotypes within media can empower children aged 8 to 10 to critically analyze messages they encounter and make informed decisions.

Understanding Advertising:

Advertising is everywhere, from television commercials to social media influencers. It is crucial to teach children to recognize when they are being marketed to and to understand the persuasive techniques used in advertisements. Discuss with them the purpose of advertising, which is often to sell a product or idea. Encourage critical thinking by asking questions like:

What is the advertiser trying to sell?

How are they trying to make the product seem appealing?

Are there any exaggerations or unrealistic portrayals?

Exploring Stereotypes:

Stereotypes are oversimplified beliefs or ideas about people based on characteristics such as gender, race, or age. In the context of sex education, media often perpetuates gender stereotypes, portraying certain behaviors or roles as typical for boys or girls. Teach children to recognize stereotypes and challenge them by:

Encouraging them to think about how people are portrayed in media.

Discussing whether these portrayals reflect real-life diversity.

Exploring how stereotypes can limit individual potential and perpetuate inequality.

Promoting Critical Media Literacy:

Media literacy empowers children to engage critically with the media they consume, helping them become informed and responsible citizens. Here are some strategies to promote media literacy in the context of sex education:

Teach children to question what they see and hear in media.

Encourage them to seek out diverse sources of information and perspectives.

Discuss the influence of media on attitudes towards sex and relationships.

Help children understand the difference between healthy and unhealthy portrayals of sexuality.

Foster open communication, so children feel comfortable asking questions and discussing their concerns.

By integrating media literacy into sex education for children aged 8 to 10, we can empower them to navigate the complex landscape of media messages surrounding sex and relationships. By understanding advertising and stereotypes, children can develop the critical thinking skills necessary to make informed decisions and form healthy attitudes towards sexuality. Ultimately, equipping children with media literacy skills prepares them to become responsible consumers and creators of media in an increasingly digital world.

Promoting Healthy Body Image

In today's digital age, children are bombarded with various media messages about body image and sexuality. As parents and educators, it's crucial to equip children with the skills to critically analyze and navigate these messages. By promoting media literacy and fostering a healthy body image, we can empower children aged 8 to 10 with the knowledge they need to make informed decisions about their bodies and relationships.

Understanding Media Literacy:

Media literacy involves understanding how media messages are constructed, interpreted, and manipulated. Children in this age group can begin to develop these skills by learning to identify different types of media (e.g., TV shows, advertisements, social media) and understanding their purposes and intended audiences. Encouraging critical thinking about media content helps children recognize stereotypes, biases, and unrealistic portrayals of body image and sexuality.

Promoting Healthy Body Image:

At this age, children are forming perceptions about their bodies and comparing themselves to societal ideals. It's essential to promote positive body image by emphasizing that bodies come in all shapes, sizes, and colors. Encourage children to appreciate their bodies for what they can do rather than how they look. Provide opportunities for physical activity and emphasize the importance of nourishing their bodies with healthy foods.

Discussing Sexuality:

Sex education at this age should focus on age-appropriate topics, such as understanding anatomical differences between boys and girls, the importance of consent and boundaries, and the concept of families. Use simple language and be open to answering questions honestly and without judgment. Emphasize the importance of respecting oneself and others in all types of relationships.

Navigating Media Messages:

Teach children to question the messages they encounter in media regarding beauty standards, gender roles, and relationships. Encourage them to ask critical questions such as: Who created this message? What are they trying to sell or promote? How does this message make me feel about myself and others? By developing these critical thinking skills, children can become more discerning consumers of media.

Practical Tips for Parents and Educators:

Co-view and discuss media content with your child, pointing out both positive and negative representations.

Encourage a diverse range of interests and hobbies to foster a well-rounded sense of self.

Model positive body image and healthy relationship behaviors in your own interactions.

Stay informed about age-appropriate resources and books that address sex education and body image.

Create a supportive environment where children feel comfortable asking questions and expressing their thoughts and feelings.

Conclusion:

By integrating media literacy and promoting healthy body image into sex education for 8 to 10-year-olds, we can empower children to navigate the complex media landscape with confidence and resilience. By fostering critical thinking skills and promoting self-acceptance, we can help them develop into informed and empowered individuals who respect themselves and others.

CHAPTER 7: BODY POSITIVITY AND SELF-CARE

Celebrating Diverse Bodies

Sex education is not just about understanding how bodies work; it's also about embracing and respecting our bodies. In this guide, we'll explore the beautiful diversity of bodies, the importance of self-care, and how to foster a positive relationship with our own bodies.

Celebrating Diverse Bodies:

Every body is unique and special in its own way. Just like there are different shapes and sizes of flowers in a garden, there are also different shapes, sizes, and colors of bodies in the world. Some people have curly hair, some have straight hair, some have freckles, and some don't. And all of these differences are what make us wonderfully unique.

It's essential to understand that there is no one "perfect" body. The media might sometimes show us images of people who look a certain way, but those are just a tiny fraction of the diversity of real bodies. In reality, bodies come in all shapes, sizes, and abilities, and they are all beautiful and worthy of love and respect.

Body Positivity:

Body positivity means loving and accepting our bodies just the way they are. It's about celebrating what makes us unique and embracing our imperfections. Instead of focusing on what we don't like about our bodies, let's focus on what we love about them. Maybe you have strong muscles that help you run fast, or maybe you have a smile that can light up a room. Whatever it is, take a moment to appreciate it.

It's also important to remember that our bodies will change as we grow older, and that's perfectly normal too. Puberty, for example, is a time when our bodies go through lots of changes, and it's important to be patient and kind to ourselves during this time. Remember, every change is a natural part of growing up, and it's nothing to be ashamed of.

Self-Care:

Taking care of our bodies is an important part of loving ourselves. Just like we need to eat healthy food to keep our bodies strong, we also need to take care of our emotional and mental well-being. This means doing things that make us feel good, like spending time with friends and family, playing outside, or doing activities we enjoy.

Self-care also means setting boundaries and saying no to things that don't make us feel good. If someone is making us feel uncomfortable or unsafe, it's okay to speak up and ask for help. Remember, your body belongs to you, and you have the right to decide what feels right for you.

By celebrating the diversity of bodies, embracing body positivity, and practicing self-care, we can learn to love and respect ourselves just the way we are. Remember, your body is amazing and deserving of love and care, no matter what it looks like. So let's celebrate our differences and embrace the beauty of diversity together.

Promoting Self-Esteem and Confidence

Sex education is about so much more than just biology and reproduction. It's about understanding and respecting our bodies, developing healthy attitudes towards ourselves and others, and cultivating positive self-esteem. In this guide, we'll explore how children aged 8 to 10 can embrace body positivity and self-care as essential components of their sexual education journey.

Understanding Body Positivity:

Body positivity is all about accepting and loving our bodies just the way they are. It's about recognizing that bodies come in all shapes, sizes, and colors, and that each one is unique and beautiful in its own way. As children grow and develop, it's important to teach them that there is no "perfect" body and that they are worthy of love and respect exactly as they are.

Promoting Self-Esteem:

Self-esteem is the way we feel about ourselves and our abilities. It's closely tied to body positivity, as having a positive body image is essential for building self-esteem. Encourage children to focus on their strengths and talents rather than comparing themselves to others. Remind them that everyone has things they're good at and that it's okay to be proud of who they are.

Practicing Self-Care:

Self-care involves taking care of our physical, emotional, and mental well-being. Teach children the importance of listening to their bodies and giving themselves the care and attention they need. This includes things like getting enough sleep, eating nutritious foods, exercising regularly, and managing stress. Help them understand that self-care isn't selfish—it's essential for leading a happy and healthy life.

Encouraging Positive Relationships:
Part of sex education is learning how to build and maintain positive relationships with others. Teach children about consent, boundaries, and respect for themselves and others. Help them understand that they have the right to say no to anything that makes them feel uncomfortable and that they should always treat others with kindness and empathy.

Challenging Stereotypes and Media Influence:

In today's world, children are bombarded with images and messages about what they should look like and how they should act. Help them develop critical thinking skills so they can challenge harmful stereotypes and media representations of beauty and masculinity/femininity. Encourage them to seek out diverse media that celebrates all kinds of bodies and identities.

Body positivity and self-care are essential components of sex education for children aged 8 to 10. By teaching them to embrace their bodies, build self-esteem, practice self-care, and cultivate positive relationships, we can empower them to navigate the complexities of growing up with confidence and resilience. Together, let's create a world where every child feels valued, accepted, and loved just the way they are.

Practicing Hygiene and Self-Care

Sex education is an essential part of growing up, and it's never too early to start learning about our bodies and how to take care of them. In this guide, we'll explore the importance of body positivity and self-care for children aged 8 to 10, helping them develop a healthy relationship with their bodies and understand the significance of hygiene.

Body Positivity:

Body positivity is all about loving and accepting our bodies just the way they are. It's essential to teach children that bodies come in all shapes, sizes, and colors, and each one is beautiful and unique. Encourage them to appreciate their own bodies and respect others' bodies, promoting a culture of acceptance and inclusivity.

Here are some ways to promote body positivity:

Focus on strengths: Encourage children to celebrate what their bodies can do rather than how they look. Whether it's running, jumping, dancing, or drawing, help them recognize and appreciate their abilities.

Positive self-talk: Teach children to speak kindly to themselves and avoid negative self-talk. Encourage them to replace self-criticism with affirmations and compliments.

Media literacy: Help children critically analyze media messages about beauty and body image.

Discuss how images in magazines, movies, and social media are often unrealistic and edited, and emphasize the importance of not comparing themselves to these unrealistic standards.

Self-Care and Hygiene:

Self-care involves taking care of our physical, mental, and emotional well-being. Hygiene, in particular, plays a crucial role in keeping our bodies healthy and clean. Here are some hygiene practices children should learn:

Bathing: Teach children the importance of bathing regularly, using soap and water to clean their bodies. Emphasize washing under the arms, behind the ears, and between the toes.

Dental care: Encourage children to brush their teeth at least twice a day and floss regularly.

Explain how proper dental hygiene prevents cavities and keeps their smiles bright.

Handwashing: Teach children the proper way to wash their hands, especially before eating, after using the bathroom, and after playing outside. Show them how to lather soap and scrub their hands for at least 20 seconds.

Changing clothes: Help children understand the importance of changing their clothes regularly, especially after sweating or getting dirty. Teach them how to put on clean underwear and socks every day.

By promoting body positivity and teaching self-care and hygiene practices, we empower children to take pride in their bodies and prioritize their well-being. By instilling these values early on, we set them on the path to a lifetime of healthy habits and positive self-image. Remember, open communication and a supportive environment are key to fostering a positive attitude towards body and self-care.

CHAPTER 8: GROWING UP IN A DIGITAL WORLD

Navigating Social Media and Online Interactions

In today's digital age, children are growing up surrounded by social media and online interactions. With the internet at their fingertips, it's crucial to equip them with the knowledge and skills to navigate these platforms safely, especially when it comes to topics like sex education. This guide is designed to empower children aged 8 to 10 with the information they need to make informed decisions and stay safe online.

Understanding Social Media:

Social media platforms like Instagram, TikTok, and Snapchat allow people to connect and share content with friends and followers. While these platforms can be fun and entertaining, it's important to understand that not everything you see online is accurate or appropriate. Sometimes people may share misleading information or post content that is not suitable for children.

Privacy and Safety:

When using social media, always prioritize your privacy and safety. Keep your personal information private and never share it with strangers online. Avoid accepting friend requests or messages from people you don't know in real life. If someone makes you feel uncomfortable or tries to pressure you into doing something you're not comfortable with, don't hesitate to block or report them.

Respecting Yourself and Others:

In the digital world, it's easy to compare yourself to others based on their online profiles. Remember that people often only show the highlights of their lives on social media, and it's okay to be yourself. Respect yourself and your body, and don't feel pressured to conform to unrealistic standards of beauty or behavior. Similarly, respect others' boundaries and privacy online.

Understanding Boundaries:

Boundaries are important both online and offline. Always ask for permission before sharing someone else's content or tagging them in posts. Respect others' boundaries when commenting or messaging them, and never engage in cyberbullying or online harassment. If you wouldn't say something to someone's face, don't say it online.

Sex Education and Consent:

As you grow older, you may encounter content online related to sex and relationships. It's essential to have a basic understanding of these topics and to know that it's okay to ask questions if you're unsure. Consent is crucial in any type of relationship, whether it's online or offline. Always respect others' boundaries and never pressure anyone into doing something they don't want to do.

Talking to Trusted Adults:

If you ever have questions or concerns about anything you see or experience online, don't hesitate to talk to a trusted adult. This could be a parent, guardian, teacher, or another responsible adult who can offer guidance and support. Remember, you're not alone, and there's always someone who cares about you and wants to help.

Growing up in a digital world presents both opportunities and challenges when it comes to navigating social media and online interactions. By understanding how to protect your privacy, respect yourself and others, and make informed decisions about sex and relationships, you can confidently navigate the digital landscape and enjoy all that the internet has to offer. Remember, you have the power to shape your online experience and make choices that reflect your values and beliefs.

Understanding Privacy and Security

In today's world, kids are growing up surrounded by technology. From smartphones to tablets, the digital landscape is vast and accessible. Alongside the endless possibilities, there are also important conversations to be had about privacy, security, and sex education. As a child between 8 to 10 years old, it's crucial to understand how to navigate this digital world responsibly. Let's explore some essential concepts:

Understanding Privacy:

Personal Information: Start by explaining what personal information is - things like your name, address, phone number, and school. Emphasize the importance of keeping this information private, especially when online.

Online Interactions: Teach kids to be cautious when interacting with others online. Explain that not everyone is who they say they are, and it's essential to never share personal information with strangers.

Privacy Settings: Introduce them to privacy settings on websites and apps. Show them how to adjust these settings to control who can see their information and posts.

Digital Security:

Passwords: Teach kids the importance of strong, unique passwords for their online accounts. Help them create secure passwords and explain why they should never share them with anyone, even friends.

Phishing: Explain what phishing is and how to recognize suspicious emails or messages. Encourage them to always verify the sender's identity before clicking on any links or providing any information.

Safe Browsing: Discuss the importance of only visiting trusted websites and downloading apps from reputable sources. Teach them to look for the padlock symbol in the browser's address bar to ensure a website is secure.

Sex Education:

Body Awareness: Start by teaching kids about their bodies and how they're changing as they grow up. Use age-appropriate language and be open to answering any questions they may have.

Boundaries: Discuss the importance of boundaries and respecting other people's boundaries. Teach them that it's okay to say no to anything that makes them uncomfortable.

Online Content: Explain that not all information online is accurate or appropriate. Encourage them to come to you with any questions or concerns they may have about things they see or hear online.

Putting it Into Practice:
Family Rules: Establish clear rules and guidelines for internet use within the family.

Encourage open communication and create a safe space for kids to ask questions or discuss any issues they encounter online.

Leading by Example: Be a positive role model for responsible digital behavior. Show kids how to use technology responsibly and respectfully.

Regular Check-ins: Schedule regular check-ins to discuss online safety and sex education. Use these opportunities to reinforce important concepts and address any new concerns that may arise.

By equipping kids with the knowledge and skills to navigate the digital world responsibly, we can help them grow into confident and informed individuals. With open communication and guidance, they can thrive in the digital age while staying safe and secure.

Promoting Digital Wellness

In today's world, where digital devices are ubiquitous, children are exposed to a plethora of information, including content related to sex and relationships. As parents and educators, it's essential to provide children aged 8 to 10 with accurate and age-appropriate sex education to help them navigate the digital landscape safely and responsibly. By promoting digital wellness and fostering open communication, we can empower children to make informed decisions and develop healthy attitudes towards sexuality.

Understanding Digital Wellness:

Digital wellness encompasses the healthy use of digital devices and online platforms. It involves balancing screen time with other activities, maintaining privacy and security online, and engaging in positive digital interactions. Incorporating sex education into the concept of digital wellness enables children to approach sexuality with a mindful and responsible attitude, ensuring their well-being in both the physical and virtual realms.

Key Topics in Sex Education for Children:
Body Awareness:

Teach children about their bodies, including anatomical terms for body parts, reproductive organs, and their functions. Encourage body positivity and self-respect by emphasizing that all bodies are unique and deserving of respect.

Healthy Relationships:

Discuss the qualities of healthy relationships, such as trust, communication, respect, and consent. Help children recognize and understand different types of relationships, including friendships, family relationships, and romantic relationships.

Consent:

Explain the concept of consent in age-appropriate terms, emphasizing that no one should touch them in a way that makes them uncomfortable. Teach them to respect others' boundaries and to speak up if they feel their boundaries are being violated.

Online Safety:

Educate children about the risks of sharing personal information online and the importance of privacy settings on social media platforms and messaging apps. Teach them to recognize and report inappropriate content or online behavior.

Media Literacy:

Help children develop critical thinking skills to evaluate the accuracy and credibility of information they encounter online, including information about sex and relationships. Encourage them to question stereotypes and unrealistic portrayals of sexuality in media and advertising.

Puberty:

Introduce the concept of puberty and the physical and emotional changes that occur during this stage of development. Offer reassurance that puberty is a normal and natural process and encourage open dialogue about any questions or concerns they may have.

Reproduction and Conception:

Provide age-appropriate information about how babies are conceived and born, including the role of sperm and eggs in reproduction. Emphasize the importance of responsible decision-making and contraception in preventing unplanned pregnancies and sexually transmitted infections (STIs).

Promoting Open Communication:

Encourage children to ask questions and express their thoughts and feelings about sex and relationships openly and without judgment. Create a safe and supportive environment where they feel comfortable seeking guidance and advice from trusted adults, such as parents, caregivers, or teachers.

By integrating sex education into the broader context of digital wellness, we can equip children with the knowledge and skills they need to navigate the digital world safely and responsibly. By promoting open communication, fostering critical thinking, and encouraging respect for oneself and others, we can empower children to develop healthy attitudes towards sexuality and relationships as they grow and mature.

CONCLUSION

In conclusion, "Sex Education for 8-12 Year Olds" offers a comprehensive guide for parents on navigating the delicate yet crucial topic of educating children about their bodies. Throughout the book, we've explored the importance of empowering children to take ownership of their bodies from an early age, fostering a healthy sense of autonomy, agency, and self-respect.

As parents, guardians, or caregivers, it's imperative to recognize that sex education encompasses far more than just the biological aspects of reproduction. It's about instilling values of consent, respect, and understanding, laying the groundwork for healthy relationships and informed decision-making as children mature.

By fostering open and honest communication channels, parents can create a supportive environment where children feel comfortable asking questions and expressing concerns about their bodies and sexuality. This communication should be ongoing, evolving with the child's age and development, and tailored to their individual needs and understanding.

Moreover, sex education should not be viewed as a one-time conversation but rather as an ongoing dialogue woven into everyday life. By integrating age-appropriate discussions about boundaries, privacy, and bodily autonomy into daily interactions, parents can reinforce these important concepts and help children develop a strong sense of self-awareness and self-worth.

In addition to parental guidance, the book emphasizes the role of schools, healthcare providers, and community resources in supporting children's sexual health and well-being. Collaborative efforts between parents, educators, and other stakeholders can ensure that children receive accurate, inclusive, and nonjudgmental information about their bodies and sexuality.

Furthermore, it's essential to recognize and respect the diversity of experiences and identities within the realm of sexuality. Children should be exposed to a broad range of perspectives, cultures, and identities, promoting empathy, understanding, and acceptance of others.

In conclusion, "Sex Education for 8-12 Year Olds" underscores the importance of empowering children to take ownership of their bodies through open communication, education, and support. By equipping children with the knowledge, skills, and confidence to navigate their evolving sexuality, parents can help them lead healthy, fulfilling lives grounded in respect, consent, and self-determination.

Dear Valued Reader,

I hope you enjoyed my book. I poured my heart and soul into it, and I'm so grateful that you took the time to read it. If you found the book helpful, insightful, or entertaining, I would be honored if you would consider leaving a positive review.

Your feedback means the world to me as an author, and it can help other potential readers discover my work. Thank you very much. God bless your kind heart. I am anticipating seeing your reviews and ratings.

Made in the USA
Middletown, DE
31 October 2024